It's Easy To Play Bach.

Wise Publications
London/New York/Sydney

DISTRIBUTED BY

HAL•LEONARD®
CORPORATION
7777 W. BLUEMOUND RD. P.O. BOX 13819 MILWAUKEE, WI 53213

Exclusive Distributors:
Music Sales Limited
8/9 Frith Street, London W1V 5TZ, England.
Music Sales Pty. Limited
120 Rothschild Avenue, Rosebery, NSW 2018, Australia.

This book © Copyright 1988 by
Wise Publications
UK ISBN 0.7119.1520.2
Order No. AM 71721

Art direction by Mike Bell
Cover illustration by Paul Leith
Compiled by Peter Evans
Arranged by Daniel Scott

Music Sales complete catalogue lists thousands
of titles and is free from your local music
book shop, or direct from Music Sales Limited.
Please send a cheque or postal order for £1.50 for postage to
Music Sales Limited, 8/9 Frith Street, London W1V 5TZ.

Air On The G String, 4
Badinerie from Suite No.2, 6
Gavotte from French Suite No.5, 8
Jesu, Joy Of Man's Desiring, 14
Largo from Concerto For Two Violins, 10
March from Anna Magdalena's Notebook, 12
Minuet from Anna Magdalena's Notebook, 18
Minuet from French Suite No.6, 22
Minuet from Partita No.1, 28
Minuet In G (Anna Magdalena), 32
Minuet 2 from Partita No.1, 36
Musette from Anna Magdalena's Notebook, 40
O Sacred Head, 30
Polonaise, 20
Prelude In C from 12 Little Preludes, 31
Prelude No.1 In C, 24
Prelude No.9, 42
Rondo from Suite No.2, 34
Sarabande, 44
Sheep May Safely Graze, 38
Wachet auf, 46

Air On The G String

Composed by Johann Sebastian Bach

Moderato

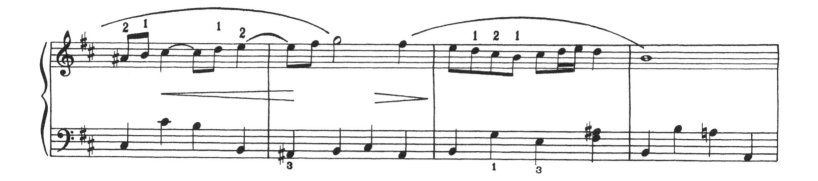

Badinerie from Suite No.2

Composed by Johann Sebastian Bach

Gavotte from French Suite No.5

Composed by Johann Sebastian Bach

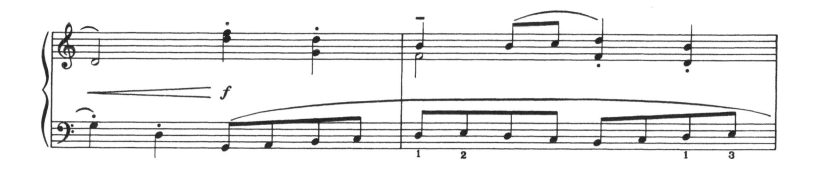

Largo from Concerto
For Two Violins

Composed by Johann Sebastian Bach

March from Anna Magdalena's Notebook

Composed by Johann Sebastian Bach

Allegro

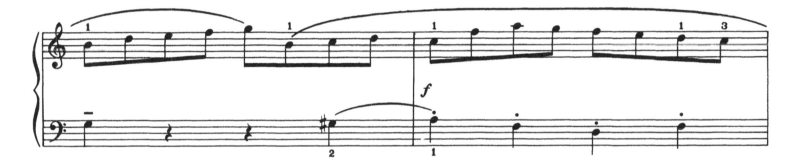

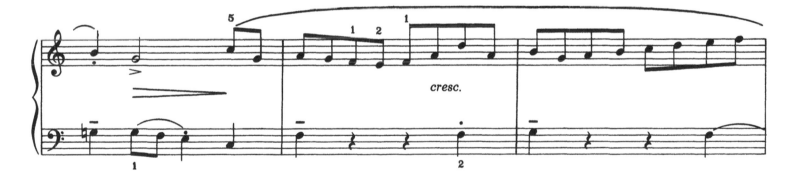

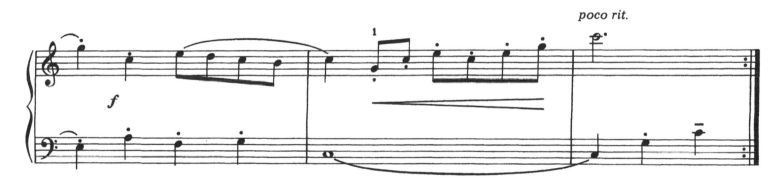

Jesu, Joy Of Man's Desiring

Composed by Johann Sebastian Bach

cresc.

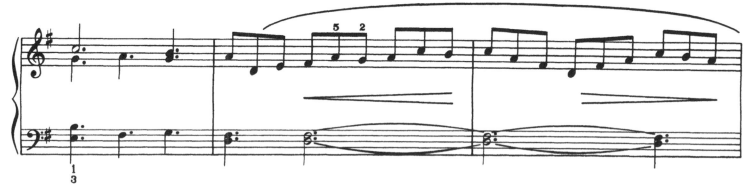

Minuet from Anna Magdalena's Notebook

Composed by Johann Sebastian Bach

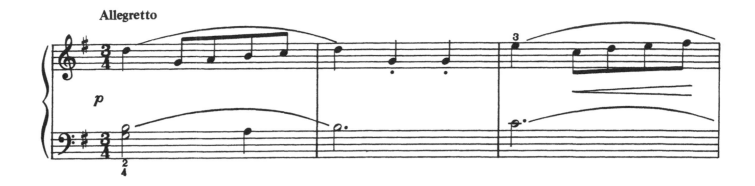

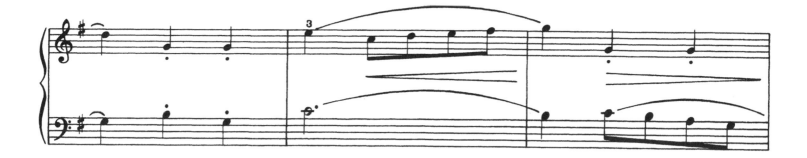

Polonaise

Composed by Johann Sebastian Bach

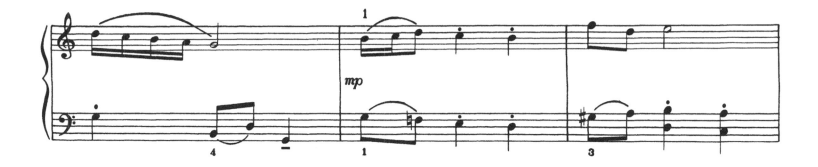

21

Minuet from French Suite No.6

Composed by Johann Sebastian Bach

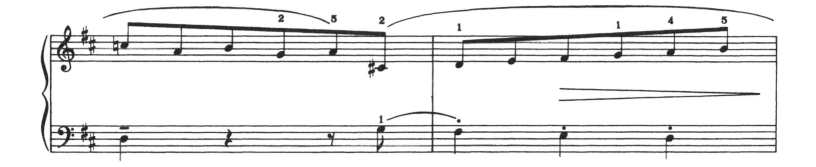

23

Prelude No.1 In C

Composed by Johann Sebastian Bach

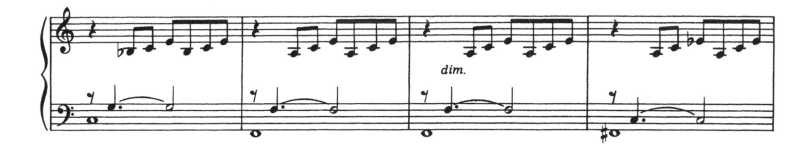

Minuet from Partita No.1

Composed by Johann Sebastian Bach

Allegretto

O Sacred Head

Composed by Johann Sebastian Bach

Hymn-like

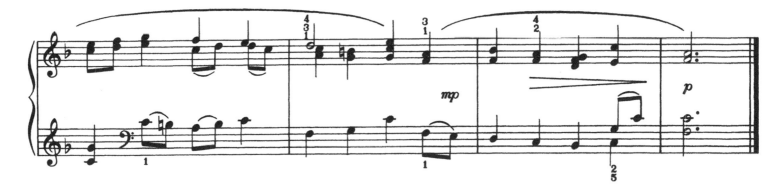

Prelude In C from 12 Little Preludes

Composed by Johann Sebastian Bach

Minuet In G (Anna Magdalena)

Composed by Johann Sebastian Bach

Allegretto

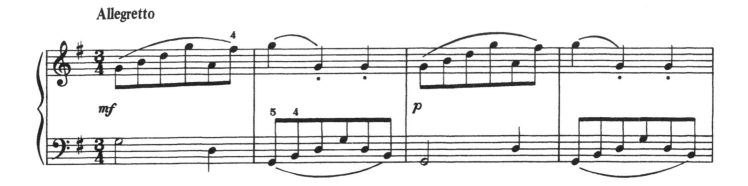

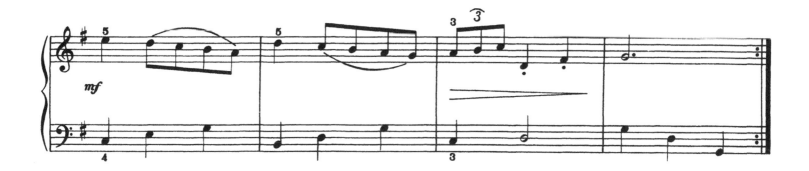

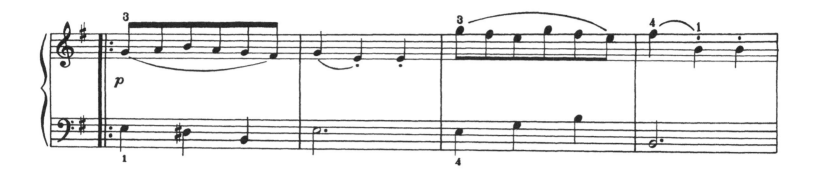

Rondo from Suite No.2

Composed by Johann Sebastian Bach

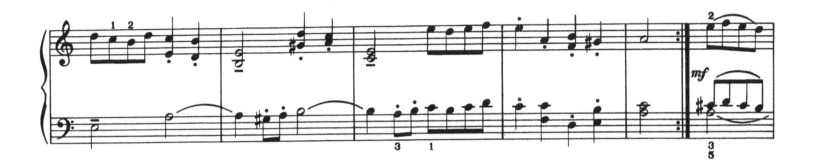

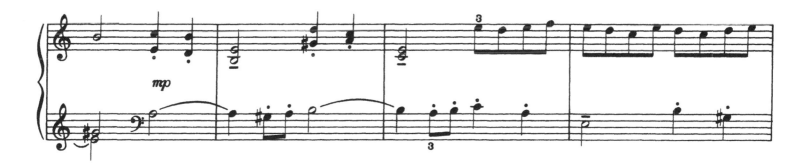

Minuet 2 from Partita No.1

Composed by Johann Sebastian Bach

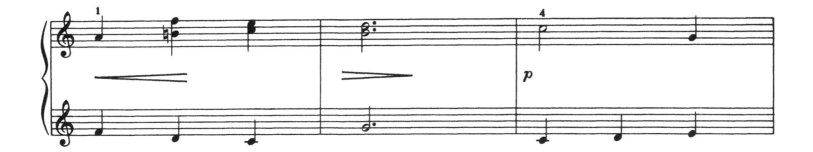

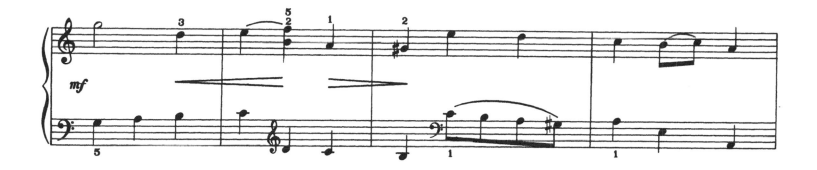

poco rit. -

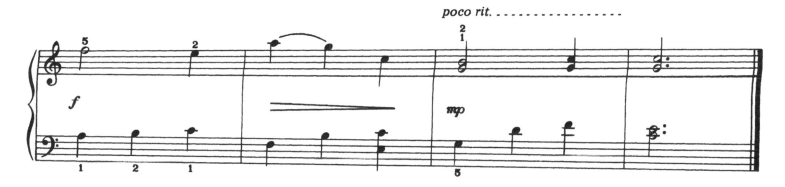

Sheep May Safely Graze

Composed by Johann Sebastian Bach

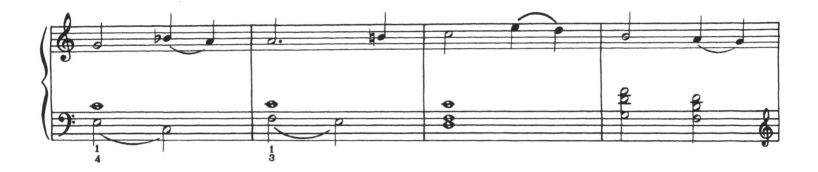

Musette from Anna Magdalena's Notebook

Composed by Johann Sebastian Bach

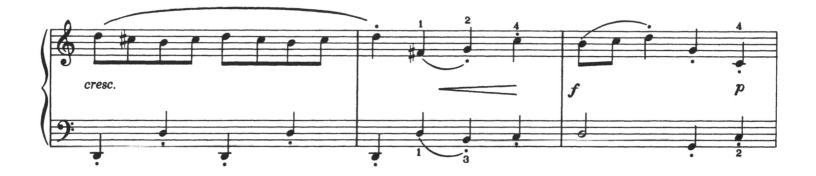

Prelude No.9

Composed by Johann Sebastian Bach

Allegretto

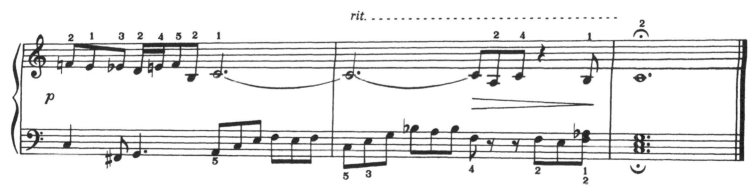

Sarabande

Composed by Johann Sebastian Bach

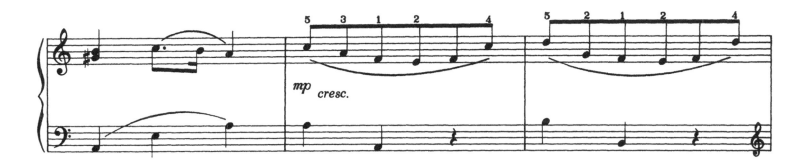

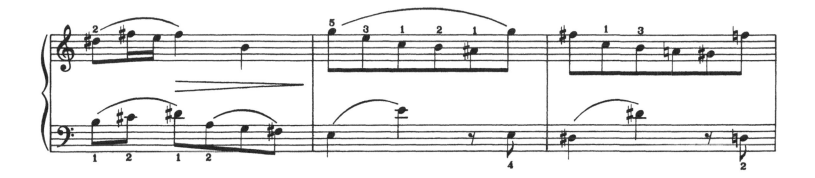

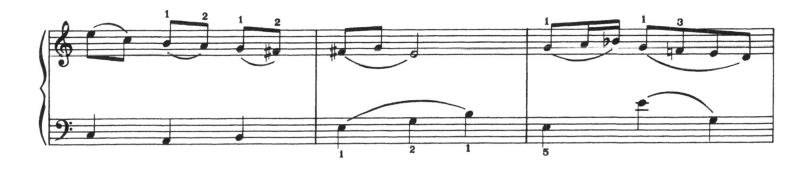

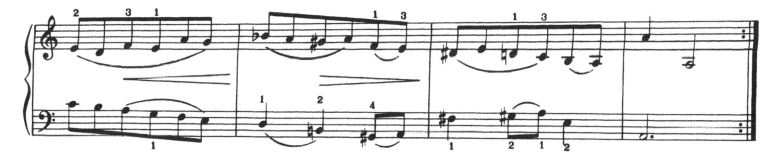

Wachet auf

Composed by Johann Sebastian Bach

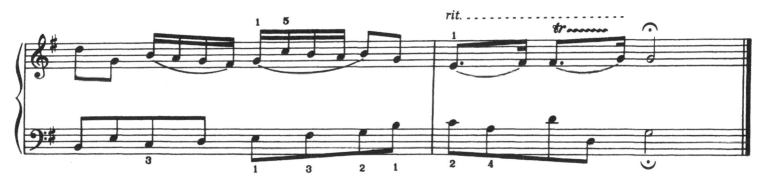

1/03 (46423)

YOUR FAVORITE MUSIC
ARRANGED FOR PIANO SOLO

ADELE FOR PIANO SOLO – 2ND EDITION

This collection features 13 Adele favorites beautifully arranged for piano solo, including: Chasing Pavements • Hello • Rolling in the Deep • Set Fire to the Rain • Someone like You • Turning Tables • When We Were Young • and more.

00307585 ....$14.99

BATTLESTAR GALACTICA

by Bear McCreary

For this special collection, McCreary himself has translated the acclaimed orchestral score into fantastic solo piano arrangements at the intermediate to advanced level. Includes 19 selections in all, and as a bonus, simplified versions of "Roslin and Adama" and "Wander My Friends." Contains a note from McCreary, as well as a biography.

00313530 ....$17.99

THE BEST JAZZ PIANO SOLOS EVER

Over 300 pages of beautiful classic jazz piano solos featuring standards in any jazz artist's repertoire. Includes: Afternoon in Paris • Giant Steps • Moonlight in Vermont • Moten Swing • A Night in Tunisia • Night Train • On Green Dolphin Street • Song for My Father • West Coast Blues • Yardbird Suite • and more.

00312079 ....$19.99

CLASSICS WITH A TOUCH OF JAZZ

Arranged by Lee Evans

27 classical masterpieces arranged in a unique and accessible jazz style. Mr Evans also provides an audio recording of each piece. Titles include: Air from Suite No. 3 (Bach) • Barcarolle "June" (Tchaikovsky) • Pavane (Faure) • Piano Sonata No. 8 "Pathetique" (Beethoven) • Reverie (Debussy) • The Swan (Saint-Saens) • and more.

00151662 Book/Online Audio...$14.99

COLDPLAY FOR PIANO SOLO

Stellar solo arrangements of a dozen smash hits from Coldplay: Clocks • Fix You • In My Place • Lost! • Paradise • The Scientist • Speed of Sound • Trouble • Up in Flames • Viva La Vida • What If • Yellow.

00307637 ....$15.99

DISNEY SONGS

12 Disney favorites in beautiful piano solo arrangements, including: Bella Notte (This Is the Night) • Can I Have This Dance • Feed the Birds • He's a Tramp • I'm Late • The Medallion Calls • Once Upon a Dream • A Spoonful of Sugar • That's How You Know • We're All in This Together • You Are the Music in Me • You'll Be in My Heart (Pop Version).

00313527 ....$14.99

GREAT THEMES FOR PIANO SOLO

Nearly 30 rich arrangements of popular themes from movies and TV shows, including: Bella's Lullaby • Chariots of Fire • Cinema Paradiso • The Godfather (Love Theme) • Hawaii Five-O Theme • Theme from "Jaws" • Theme from "Jurassic Park" • Linus and Lucy • The Pink Panther • Twilight Zone Main Title • and more.

00312102 ....$14.99

PRIDE & PREJUDICE

12 piano pieces from the 2006 Oscar-nominated film, including: Another Dance • Darcy's Letter • Georgiana • Leaving Netherfield • Liz on Top of the World • Meryton Townhall • The Secret Life of Daydreams • Stars and Butterflies • and more.

00313327 ....$17.99

GEORGE GERSHWIN – RHAPSODY IN BLUE (ORIGINAL)

Alfred Publishing Co.

George Gershwin's own piano solo arrangement of his classic contemporary masterpiece for piano and orchestra. This masterful measure-for-measure two-hand adaptation of the complete modern concerto for piano and orchestra incorporates all orchestral parts and piano passages into two staves while retaining the clarity, sonority, and brilliance of the original.

00321589 ....$16.99

ROMANTIC FILM MUSIC

40 piano solo arrangements of beloved songs from the silver screen, including: Anyone at All • Come What May • Glory of Love • I See the Light • I Will Always Love You • Iris • It Had to Be You • Nobody Does It Better • She • Take My Breath Away (Love Theme) • A Thousand Years • Up Where We Belong • When You Love Someone • The Wind Beneath My Wings • and many more.

00122112 ....$17.99

STAR WARS: THE FORCE AWAKENS

Music from the soundtrack to the seventh installment of the Star Wars® franchise by John Williams is presented in this songbook, complete with artwork from the film throughout the whole book, including eight pages in full color! Titles include: The Scavenger • Rey Meets BB-8 • Rey's Theme • That Girl with the Staff • Finn's Confession • The Starkiller • March of the Resistance • Torn Apart • and more.

00154451 ....$17.99

TAYLOR SWIFT FOR PIANO SOLO – 2ND EDITION

This updated second edition features 15 of Taylor's biggest hits from her self-titled first album all the way through her pop breakthrough album, *1989*. Includes: Back to December • Blank Space • Fifteen • I Knew You Were Trouble • Love Story • Mean • Mine • Picture to Burn • Shake It Off • Teardrops on My Guitar • 22 • We Are Never Ever Getting Back Together • White Horse • Wildest Dreams • You Belong with Me.

00307375 ....$16.99

UP

Music by Michael Giacchino

Piano solo arrangements of 13 pieces from Pixar's mammoth animated hit: Carl Goes Up • It's Just a House • Kevin Beak'n • Married Life • Memories Can Weigh You Down • The Nickel Tour • Paradise Found • The Small Mailman Returns • The Spirit of Adventure • Stuff We Did • We're in the Club Now • and more, plus a special section of full-color artwork from the film!

00313471 ....$17.99

HAL•LEONARD®

7777 W. BLUEMOUND RD. P.O. BOX 13819 MILWAUKEE, WI 53213

www.halleonard.com